FINDING YOUR WAY

through

Divorce

Finding Your Way through Divorce is a must read for Catholics who are experiencing the trauma of divorce. Speaking from her experience, Kathy Brewer Gorham explains the grief to growth process as necessary for a new lifestyle. If the process is short-circuited because the person ignores or minimizes it, the individual experiencing divorce will not grow into a hopeful future.

Rev. Vincent O'Brien, S.J.
Former International Chaplain for the North American Conference of Separated and Divorced Catholics

Gorham's insightful, prayerful, and intuitive guide helps Christians travel the rocky emotional landscape of divorce. Her reliance on faith, paired with her realistic and empathetic portrayal of Christian divorce makes this a book that will offer salve to many.

Brette McWhorter Sember
Author of *No-Fight Divorce*

As Catholics, we are taught the sacramentality of marriage, but, as humans, we experience the pain of failure through divorce. *Finding Your Way through Divorce* prayerfully leads the reader through the many emotions and behaviors accompanying divorce and into the loving arms of our merciful Christ.

Irene M. Varley, M.A.
Executive Director
North American Conference of Separated and Divorced Catholics

FINDING YOUR WAY

through

Divorce

Kathy Brewer Gorham

ave maria press AMP notre dame, indiana

Founded in 1865, Ave Maria Press is a ministry of the Indiana Province of Holy Cross.

www.avemariapress.com

ISBN-10 1-59471-074-0 ISBN-13 978-1-59471-074-2

Cover and text design by Brian C. Conley

Printed and bound in the United States of America.

Library of Congress Cataloging-in-Publication Data
Gorham, Kathy Brewer.
Finding your way through divorce / Kathy Brewer Gorham.
p. cm.
ISBN-13: 978-1-59471-074-2 (pbk.)
ISBN-10: 1-59471-074-0 (pbk.)
1. Divorce--Religious aspects--Catholic Church. I. Title.

BX2254.G67 2006
248.8'46--dc22

2006007277

Acknowledgments

Finding Your Way through Divorce was influenced by hundreds of divorced men and women who I met on my divorce journey or whose stories I heard from leaders of the North American Conference of Separated and Divorced Catholics groups while I was Executive Director. I want to thank those who shared their pain, hopes, and dreams with me. It has been an honor.

I would like to thank the North American Conference of Separated and Divorced Catholics for giving me the confidence and knowledge to become the person I am now. *Finding Your Way through Divorce* would never have been published without them.

My deepest gratitude goes to those who encouraged a new writer, assuring me that my words had a message to all the hurting separated and divorced Christians:

my husband, MERRILL,

my daughters, KRISTA AND ANGIE, my six stepchildren,

...and

SISTER MARIETTA SCHINDLER
SISTER ALBERTA DIEKER
JANET GLISSON
CARRIE HANSEN
FR. VINCE O'BRIEN

A special thanks to those who helped in proofreading:

SUE SCHLIESKI
THERESA BEERY
JEANNETTE BIEKER
JANIS BOZARTH

Contents

preface

Divorce is one of the most devastating types of grief you will ever encounter. Unless it has happened to you, you have no idea what an overwhelming emotional time it is. I know, because I have been through it. It took me years to work through the healing process. Sometimes I felt like it was one step forward and two steps back.

I tried to ignore my grief and believed that it would eventually go away. I prayed that God would take my former husband so I wouldn't have to face the divorce. At first I was convinced the solution to my pain was to find a new love. Luckily for me, I learned in a hurry that this was not the answer.

Like many of you, I was not aware that there were organizations willing to help me through this crisis. My parish priest gave me information from the North American Conference of Separated and Divorced Catholics. Because there was not a support group where I lived, I drove two hundred and fifty miles to diocesan group meetings until I was ready to start a local group. Being a group leader for years and ending up as Executive Director of the organization, I heard many stories from divorced men and women. The stories illustrated here are real stories of divorced people who know what it is like to feel hopeless and alone. To protect their privacy, I've used fictitious names, and some of the details of the stories have been altered to hide the individual identities.

Finding Your Way through Divorce was written in the hope that you would use this book as a resource to recover from the trauma and become a better person. You may ask, "How will I ever recover from the gut wrenching pain I feel?" Well, believe me, it is a long process, but you can recover and grow from the experience if you do your grief work. There is hope. I have seen God work miracles in people who gave up on him. He may do more for you in the next two or three years than he has accomplished in the past ten years. I have seen people grow from being a scared mouse to a roaring lion.

Just reading *Finding Your Way through Divorce* does not mean you will suddenly be healed after the last page. Divorce recovery is a long process. By reading this book, answering the questions, and finding help (either through a professional or support group), you will gain the tools you need to begin the journey and stay on the road to healing.

Recovery is best achieved when you have someone to bounce your feelings off of. If there is not a support group available near you, find a friend who is also going through a divorce, someone who would be willing to meet with you once or twice a month to read each chapter and answer the questions. You may want to spend more than one session on some subjects. Remember, you may bounce from one emotion to another and back again. It is helpful if at these times you repeat some of the vignettes.

A few comments about my writing style: I blend theory, stories, and spiritual components to make each chapter interesting, to teach you valuable tools for recovery, and to deepen your faith in God. When you experience the anger, guilt, and bitterness of divorce, you may wonder if God is really out there, if he really cares. Sometimes you may lose your faith for a while. During these times you may want to skip the prayers at the end of each chapter, but I encourage you to just read them through. God never ceases to love you, and someday you will be able to feel his love again.

In early stages of grief it may be hard to concentrate for long periods of time, so each chapter is short, for easy reading. I hope you will find this helpful. You will also find that some chapters are similar in content. This is done so that you can closely analyze your emotions, and your story, which needs to be told over and over again.

If you take the time to read *Finding Your Way through Divorce* and process the questions from the end of each chapter, it will go a long way toward helping you out of your current crisis. God bless you and your family during this time of transition.

1

feeling pain: surviving divorce

A time to weep, and a time to laugh;
a time to mourn, and a time to dance.
—ECCLESIASTES 3:4 (NRSV)

Jerry woke up each morning hoping that he would be living someone else's life, because he absolutely hated his. The pain was so extreme, and it never left him. He would wake up with the pain each morning and go to sleep with it each night. Wasn't there a quick fix to divorce agony?

Divorce is like a hurricane. It shreds your life into small little pieces and threatens to destroy everything in its path. The emotional whirlwind of a divorce, like a hurricane, brings fear, confusion, and despair, affecting you and everyone around you. You, like so many hurricane evacuees, may ask "Why did God let this storm hit my life? Why does it hurt so much? Will the pain ever go away?" It is easier to clean up the damage of a hurricane than it is to clean up the damage caused by a divorce. Divorce is one of the most painful experiences you can go through, because it impacts every aspect of your life. You may think there is an easy way out, or a quick fix. But the truth is there is no shortcut to a pain-free divorce. Healing is a process, a moment by moment, day by day, week by week, month by month, and yes, even year by year process. How you survive the divorce depends on you. You can simply go through the divorce or you can grow through it. It's your decision.

How do you grow through divorce to become a better person?

Ask God for help.

- Find a local divorce recovery group where you can share what you are feeling with others who are going through the same pain.
- You should consider a few sessions with a good therapist. Don't give up if you are not comfortable with the first therapist after two or three sessions. Find another therapist. It is extremely important that you feel comfortable, safe, and understood.
- Avoid substance abuse as a way to temporarily minimize your pain.
- Remember grief has no time limit. Do not let others influence the duration of your grieving.
- Pray through this book. Answer the questions honestly and come back to them periodically.

Reflective Questions:

1. Can you relate to Jerry when he says he wishes he was living someone else's life? Whose life do you wish you could be living and why?

2. Describe the pain that you are feeling from your divorce.

3. How are you dealing with that pain?

Asking for God's Help:

Dear Jesus, my life is ripped apart. No one knows what I am feeling except you. Help me to rely on you. Everywhere I turn I focus on the devastation and pain of the divorce. It consumes my very being. I can't think straight and I'm so afraid. Help me to remember that you are not going to give me more than I can handle, that you are always at my side. Thank you for understanding me and loving me as I am. Amen.

2

feeling emotional: mood swings

I waited patiently for the LORD; he inclined to me and heard my cry.
—PSALM 40:1 (NRSV)

Julie sits in her easy chair day after day, unable to function. Ordinarily very active, Julie now finds herself incapable of doing even the simplest household chores. She finds herself awake most of the night, reliving every moment of the past few weeks. Julie wonders why she didn't see this coming and what she could have done to prevent it. Julie dreamed of growing old together with Jim. She never considered that she would ever be single again. She does not want to be single again. She hates being alone. A tremendous amount of fear comes over Julie at the thought of being alone forever. Julie thinks that it would be easier if Jim had died. If she was a widow she wouldn't have to tell everyone that she had failed as a wife. The church would accept her as a widow, but would she be accepted as a divorcee? "I do not want to live without him," Julie pleads with God. "Is there meaning to my life without a husband? Am I still a whole person?"

Like Julie, at some point during your "crazy period," you may experience scary emotional mood swings. Emotions of all sorts begin to emerge and can almost eliminate your ability to function. Fear is so real you can taste it. Sadness is so deep that you will wonder if you will ever be happy again. Anger is so strong that, like Julie, you may even think that you would be better off if your spouse wasn't around anymore, or you may contemplate suicide. These emotions come and go, threatening to overtake or destroy you. When these emotions seem to overcome you, *seek help*. Call a friend, a relative, or a therapist and tell them what you are feeling. Making a few appointments with a therapist is a good idea when you are in this crazy time.

The emotional pain of divorce is real. In fact, it is so real, and so painful, that you may try to ignore it or deny it. Instead, think of this emotional pain as a broken leg. Ignoring the pain and going about life as if nothing were wrong could be fatal. If the leg was allowed to heal unattended by a physician, it most likely would heal in a deformed manner, and thus impair your movement for the rest of your life. Like a broken leg, if grief is ignored it can result in prolonging and intensifying your healing process. The emotional pain may reveal itself in different ways, such as anger toward your children or your co-workers, drinking obsessively, or abusing drugs. If you did break your leg, you would seek help from a physician. The emotional pain of divorce also needs tending to if you want to heal and live a healthy life again.

Reflective Questions:

1. What emotions are you feeling which keep you from doing your everyday tasks at home or at work?

2. Name three people with whom you have discussed these emotions. Did discussing these emotions help? How?

Asking for God's Help:

Be with me Jesus, as I seek strength to get through this crazy time. I pray that I will have the courage to keep my fears and anger under control. When I'm letting my emotions get the best of me, please pull me back to reality. Help me to accept the fact that I might need to seek help from a therapist or counselor, to understand that it is okay to need help, and to believe that what I am feeling is normal. Thank you for understanding my needs and being with me during this awful time of my life. Amen.

3

feeling crazy: being "normal"

I cried out to God for help;
I cried out to God to hear me.
—PSALM 77:1 (NIV)

Jody could not believe it when she found out her husband had rented an apartment for himself and his girlfriend. She and Jim had been happily married for twenty-five years, or at least she thought that was the case. The signs were always good. He was attentive to her: small but important things, like having breakfast and coffee ready for her in the morning, or cleaning the snow and ice off her car before going to work. He loved her. How could this happen? It wasn't happening. It was a nightmare.

Jody decided she would do anything to keep him: lose weight, get a better job. "Let's go on a vacation together and everything will be better when we come home," she pleaded. They took the vacation and nothing changed. Jim left and never returned.

Jody started living the "crazy time" of divorce. At work she functioned only because she had people to talk to. At home she sat alone in her easy chair with her coat on. Fixing dinner was the farthest thing from her mind. Her mail and paper were left unread. Jody slept in her clothes in the chair for many nights. Friends would stop by to feed her and help her to bed. This lasted for a month or two. This was crazy time.

"Crazy" pretty well explains the emotions that you will experience the first few months of your divorce. You will have feelings of numbness, hopelessness, and loss. You will be mad at everyone and everything, and have a general feeling of helplessness and confusion. There will be recurring questions: "Am I ever going to feel normal again? Will this hurt ever stop? What did I do to deserve this? What can I do to make my spouse come back to me?"

If you can relate to Jody, be patient with yourself. Ask for and accept help. Accept your feelings as normal. Talk to someone about your feelings; don't stuff them away. It's okay to seek help from a professional for a while. Many cities have divorce support groups. These groups help because the people involved have all been where you are. It's a great place to retell your story over and over again. Be careful during this crazy time that you do not abuse alcohol or drugs. Grief work is done best when you are fully attentive to your feelings.

During this crazy time your grief over the loss of your relationship may manifest itself in many stages. These stages may occur repeatedly, in no certain order, and without patterns. Just remember that these are normal feelings.

Reflective Questions:

1. Write a short story explaining how you found out about your divorce.

2. What are your feelings about the divorce at this moment?

Angry,	hurt,	abandoned,	bitter,	cheated,	embarrassed?
Rejected,	sad,	resentful,	relieved,	indifferent,	overwhelmed?
Guilty,	sorry,	exhausted,	confused,	supported,	grateful?

Asking for God's Help:

Lord Jesus, be with me as I go through this miserable crazy time. Help me to remember that what I am feeling is normal. Give me the strength to face what lies ahead for me. Help me to start believing in myself and others again. Thank you for all the loved ones who listen to my story and don't judge me. Thank you for loving me even though I sometimes don't love myself. I need you by my side. Amen.

4

feeling hurt: identifying feelings

Be merciful to me, LORD, for I am faint;
O LORD heal me. . . .
—PSALM 6:2 (NIV)

Jessie was not prepared for the deep hurt she felt when Steve left her. "There's no way anyone can survive this kind of hurt and live," thought Jessie. It was the most excruciating pain she had ever experienced. Jessie kept thinking that she didn't want to live if she had to live without Steve. Jessie would often pray to God to take her life.

The pain of divorce is much worse than most people imagine, because it is the loss of all your hopes and dreams. It is the end of the life as you and your family have known it. You may have feelings of fear, blame, rejection, loneliness, and anger. The list can go on and on. All of these emotions are like a seething pot which can lead to deep depression and despair. The hurt that you are feeling is beyond the comprehension of anyone who has not been through a divorce.

Friends and family mean well when they try to help by telling you not to feel the way you are feeling, that you are okay, you just need to find someone else. They do not understand how this devastation affects you emotionally, physically, mentally, and spiritually. You must identify and face your feelings in order to move beyond this pain. It is far more helpful to be able to say, for example, "I'm sad," or "I'm angry," than it is to allow your feelings to smolder and then ignite into flames at an inappropriate time. Using words to express feelings is a far better way of dealing with your emotions than allowing your anger to be acted out in the workplace or at home with your children. Learning to deal with your feelings so they don't overwhelm you is an important skill you must develop.

Communicating your feelings verbally will open you up to grieve your loss, so that the issues causing your feelings can be resolved sooner. Begin by accepting that feelings are okay and that there are no right or wrong feelings, unless you act on them immorally (i.e., hurting someone physically). You cannot control your feelings, but you can control your actions surrounding them.

Reflective Questions:

1. Keep a daily written list of your feelings. Keep this list ongoing for about a month. This will help you to learn what you are feeling at certain points and may help you discover why you feel that way.

2. What feelings were you not allowed to experience or express when you were a child?

3. What feelings give you the most trouble right now? Why do you think that these particular feelings are more difficult for you to handle?

Asking for God's Help:

Loving Jesus, you know exactly how I feel. Please rescue me. Hold me in your arms. Comfort me as I deal with feelings that sometimes scare me. Help me to allow myself to feel these emotions so that I can better understand myself and start on my healing journey. Heal me as only you can, and guide me in taking one step forward each day. Keep me from putting my feelings into actions that would cause hurt to other people. Amen.

5

feeling alone: moving beyond alienation

Though my father and mother forsake me,
the LORD *will receive me.*

—PSALM 27:10 (NIV)

When Dave finally found the courage to inform his family and friends that Sally had left him, he thought he would receive support and encouragement from them. But his family and friends reacted the opposite way. They backed away and treated him like a failure and a loser. Even in church he felt alone. He not only lost his wife, but he felt his whole world had deserted him. Being divorced was bad enough, but to have his family, friends, and church turn against him made the trauma of divorce even worse. Dave felt isolated and alone. He felt like he was wearing a big scarlet "D" on his chest. Dave's married friends didn't want him around any more. He never thought they would react like this.

Dave's old friends didn't really know what to do with him, so they often did nothing. His friends were Sally's friends too, so they didn't want to take sides. They felt uncomfortable with him as a newly single friend among the old married couples, so they handled their discomfort by ignoring him.

You may think everyone else in church lives in a wonderful happy family and that you don't belong there anymore. You are sitting there in sorrow and dying inside. This makes you feel very distant from everyone and like you cannot connect with these people anymore. They do not understand the pain and emotional suffering you are going through. This is a normal reaction for a person going through separation or divorce. You are not alone in these feelings, so do not let your confusing emotions worry you. You do belong there and God wants you to continue to come and be with him in his church. Even if you find that some people in church make you feel alienated, your local church family is the best opportunity to find help and support. God had no intentions for a man or woman to be disassociated from other people, especially his family. God does not want you to be apart from him. He loves you unconditionally. When you feel alienated, realize that it might be a good time to find others in your church that are in the same predicament.

Same-sex friendships may keep you from plunging into a shallow romantic relationship, which most likely will end up making you feel more rejected and unwanted. Friendships of any kind take time and energy; they require you to be a giver and a listener, not just a taker and a talker. Friendship involves personal sacrifice, but the rewards are tremendous. Seek out friends who build you up; avoid ones who don't help you to be healthy.

You may need to re-learn how to begin new relationships and to build the depth necessary to support your needs and expectations. New aspirations and attitudes may be established and new life patterns may be created as you discover new means of meeting needs and reaching goals. Yet, this is not an emotionally stable time. You may face desperate loneliness.

Dave joined a divorce recovery group in his parish, and it became his family. This was a place where he belonged, where he could tell people how he felt, and knew they understood. They became his family because of shared pain. A church support group could be helpful to you, too. These groups provide a safe place where you can share your hurts, your concerns, and your fears with other people who are in the divorce recovery process. These people can best relate to what you are going through, and the facilitators of these support groups, who have typically been through a divorce themselves, are in a position to give you spiritual guidance.

REFLECTIVE QUESTIONS:

1. Can you relate to Dave's story of alienation by his married friends and church?

2. What are some ways you are dealing with or could deal with alienation?

3. Make a sign for your bathroom mirror that says "Take one day at a time."

ASKING FOR GOD'S HELP:

My Lord Jesus, help me to realize that you are not rejecting me. Help me to open my heart to you and to others who are trying to help me through this time of loneliness and pain. Give me reassurance that I can find friends and hope in the church. Thank you for giving me friends with whom I can share my story. They have survived some of the same feelings I am feeling. Help me to find more friends of my own sex to talk and share with. Amen.

6

feeling depressed: knowing and liking yourself

He heals the broken-hearted
and binds up their wounds.
—PSALM 147:3 (NRSV)

Ginger thought that if she was constantly with others she wouldn't have to face the tragedy of her divorce. She hated being alone. So, every evening after work she would go with someone to the local hangouts. But in the morning, when she was faced with the fact that she was alone, she would get severely depressed. Some mornings the depression was so bad that she couldn't make it to work. This went on until a friend told her about a singles group just for women, where they worked on getting to know themselves better and learning to live alone and like it. Ginger attended the singles group a few times, but she still thought the best answer was dating. After many failed relationships and many nights crying herself to sleep, she decided to try to make the singles group a priority. Little by little, she felt herself growing and liking herself more and more. She enjoyed getting out with the girls and just being silly and having fun. Ginger realized that by getting to know herself and liking who she was, she was preparing herself for dating later on if she wished to.

Dating during the early stages of the divorce recovery process should be done very cautiously. Rather than doing lots of dating at this point, substantial energy should be given to being alone or to building same-sex friendship networks. Same-sex friends can provide you with emotional stability and keep you from making poor choices. They can help build up your self-awareness. They teach you what's good about yourself, how you can grow, and how you can be all that God wants you to be.

Some divorced people rapidly attach themselves to someone of the opposite sex. They feel it's better to be with someone during this time. The result of this attachment is almost always another letdown, but many people have to discover this for themselves. Being in a relationship is like novocaine in a dentist's office: It temporarily dulls the pain of the divorce. In reality, jumping into another relationship at this time only postpones much of the grief and sadness they will eventually have to face.

The early stages of the divorce recovery process are a risky time to seek new romantic relationships. There is yet far too much mending and healing to do. There is no quick way to pass through the divorce recovery process. Those who attempt to deny the impact or the reality of the loss are bound to make the same mistakes over and over again.

You may have heard the saying, "Don't go shopping when you're hungry." It is because you will always pick out things that are not good for you. The same is true for getting attached too early in the recovery stage of divorce. The point is, if you hope to successfully remarry in the future, then it is of paramount importance that you do not date until you are emotionally healed, and then take dating very, very slowly. Attempting to do so too early is a big mistake.

This is the best time for you to find out what *you* like to do. Think back to when you were younger. What did you enjoy most? Skiing? Singing? Playing an instrument? All these pleasures are at your fingertips once more. Have fun with the adventure of getting to know who you are. Like Ginger, you may really start to like the person you are.

Reflective Questions:

1. Why do you think dating could be potentially dangerous as you go through the divorce recovery?

2. Make a list of activities that you would like to try (for example, dancing, learning to play an instrument, traveling, etc.). Choose one and make a plan to help you try it. Then make your plan into reality!

3. Some believe that for every five years that you were married, you need one year of recovery before you are ready for a new relationship. What do you think?

ASKING FOR GOD'S HELP:

Dear Father, guide me today to seek out new friends who will help me to grow closer to you and to improve myself so that someday I may be ready for another romantic relationship. Help me to be a friend to others also. Amen.

7

feeling numb: an emotional distance

I am weary with my moaning;
every night I flood my bed with tears;
I drench my couch with my weeping.
—PSALM 6:6 (NRSV)

Laura started missing days at work, which was very unusual for her. She declined lunch dates, which only a month ago she would have jumped at. Laura once enjoyed meeting friends after work or talking for hours to them on the phone. Now she will not answer her phone. Friends and family are worried about her but don't know how to help. You see, Laura just found out her husband wants out of their marriage.

You may be like Laura, going through the first emotions of divorce. Shock frequently begins the grieving process with any major loss. Loss is at times so overwhelming that, like Laura, you may go into "protection mode" for a time. This protection mode includes shock, numbness, difficulty with short-term memory, physical distress, and sometimes confusion. "What? This is happening to me? How could it be true? I must be having a bad dream. Surely I'll wake up in the morning and find out it's just a dream."

You may react in many different ways in a state of shock. Like Laura, you too may withdraw into a shell and block out all thoughts of what is happening. She was protecting herself from the deep trauma that the divorce caused. Laura thought that if she ignored everyone and everything, the divorce wouldn't happen. Or, you may be like Dave, who thought that if he went on with life like nothing happened, he would not end up in divorce court. This kept him from dealing with the sorrow that he would ultimately have to face. Shock provides temporary emotional distance in order to allow you to absorb the overwhelming sorrow, anger, or fear more slowly.

Not everyone going through divorce faces shock. If you initiated the divorce the real shock may have occurred several years previously, when it became apparent that a divorce was imminent. In some cases the shock is the result of being physically abused, or finding out your spouse is having an affair.

However, if you never realized that your marriage was in trouble until the day your spouse walked out, that is when your body's natural defense mechanism kicked in to protect you from the reality of the situation. That is when you entered the shock stage. Yes, you do have to face the reality of your situation at some point, but during the initial days of your trauma your body is specially designed to let you deal with only a small number of things at a time.

If there are children in the marriage, they also face shock. Be as honest as you can with them without including upsetting details. Reassure them that they are loved by both parents. Excluding them from what is going on around them, even if you think they are too young to understand, could be detrimental to their emotional development. If you feel you cannot face your children, find someone who can help you explain things to them.

Reflective Questions:

1. How did shock help you get through the early weeks of your divorce?

2. What methods have you found helpful to console your children (if you have them)?

Asking for God's Help:

Loving Jesus, why am I hurting so much? Why do you allow this pain to continue? I thought that you wouldn't give me more than I can handle, but I'm not so sure about this time. Help me to continue to have faith that I can handle this and that you are always there to help me. Help my children, who are also going through this tragedy. Thank you for letting me vent my hurt and anger to you. Amen.

8

feeling desperate: the bargaining stage

For you are the God in whom I take refuge; why have you cast me off? Why must I walk about mournfully because of the oppression of the enemy?

—PSALM 43:2 (NRSV)

Cathy was depressed and lonely. She hated the single life that she was thrown into after her separation from Ralph. How could she make the pain in her heart go away? She concluded that if she could manipulate Ralph into coming back home, everything would be great. She called Ralph and bargained with him that she would lose weight and get a job if he would just move back into the house with her. She pleaded with her in-laws to talk to their son about moving back in with her, for the children's sake. If she had to raise these kids alone, she would have to move far away and they wouldn't see them but once or twice a year. Cathy would spend hours dressing up before Ralph came to pick up the kids just to show him how much weight she had lost and how much younger-looking she was. She felt guilty that she hadn't taken care of herself all the years she and Ralph had been married. Cathy was in the bargaining stage of divorce recovery.

During this stage, most people are hurting so much that they are willing to try anything to get the hurt to stop. Such desperation can make you seek relief in drugs, alcohol, or shallow relationships. You fantasize about making deals with your former spouse or God to fix everything. "God, I will give half of everything I own to the poor if you will just let him come back to me." Sometimes bargaining is an attempt to save your marriage; other times it's to save your self-esteem. But most often, it is an attempt to postpone the inevitable. Bargaining is a stage of making deals with the world in order to avoid the pain. It's a combination stage where you deal with your own assurance of acceptability and also attempt to make changes in order to win your spouse back into your life. This is the stage where women tend to dress more attractively and act sexier. Women who never wore makeup before will now not leave the house without it. Men get new cars, wear clothes that they never would have worn before the divorce, start jogging or join a gym, and go out to the hot spots in town. This is the "if only" stage.

At the bargaining stage, you may be wrestling with damaged self-esteem. You'll try to prove to yourself and to others that you are still appealing and still have self-worth. You may be trying on a new identity, because you feel the old one didn't work. This is a normal process during this stage.

Sometimes bargains work, but most often they don't. And if they seem to work at first, in a few months it's back to the same old stuff again. You haven't gained anything—except lower self-esteem—because you failed once again. Most of the time you come to the sad realization that your best attempt at negotiations accomplished nothing.

Is bargaining with God wrong? Even Jesus in his humanity bargained with his heavenly father the night before he died. He prayed, "Abba, Father . . . all things are possible for you. Take this cup away from me." But Jesus, in his time of sorrow and fear, trusted his father and said, "Not what I will but what you will"(Mk 14:36).

Bargaining may be a last-ditch attempt to try to control your life so that it will end up your way. It is the final effort to hold on to what is important to you or what you now think is important for you. You are trying in every way humanly possible to ease the pain you are feeling. But you must be careful not to lose your values, your self-esteem, your faith, or your future in the bargaining process. This phase of grief is often the briefest of all the stages.

Reflective Questions:

1. Have you tried to bargain with God or your former spouse? Explain.

2. When you were bargaining, was it to save the marriage or to save your self-esteem?

3. Make a sign and tape it to your mirror that says, "I am very lovable." Read it out loud every time you see it.

Asking for God's Help:

Jesus, you know how I feel, because you went through these feelings when you were in the garden of Gethsemane. Help me to have faith in our heavenly father like you did and be able to say, "Not my will but yours, Lord." Work with me when I feel there is no hope and I want to give up. Be with me when I feel abandoned and alone. Open my heart so that I can give up my control of this divorce and give control back to you. Help me to accept everyone as you accept me in my weaknesses. Keep reminding me that I am lovable. Amen.

9

feeling confused: the power of denial

Hear, O LORD, and be gracious to me!
O LORD, be my helper!
—PSALM 30:10 (NRSV)

John returned from a business trip to find an empty house and a letter explaining that, since their youngest was on her way to college, there was no reason for his wife to stay around. No reason? John was confused. Ann had been his wife for twenty-eight years. She was his high school sweetheart and he loved her even more now. John thought she felt the same way.

A few days later, Ann called to see how he was doing. He questioned her about why she was doing this to him. She explained that twenty-eight years ago she made a big mistake by getting married. Ann wanted out of her parents' house and thought marriage was the only way out, and John was willing to marry her.

Ann continued by saying that she thought at that time she would someday fall in love with him. After the three children came along, she couldn't see a way out. Ann told John she did love him but wasn't in love with him. That was all he needed to hear. He was oblivious to everything else. She loved him. She would be back. Nothing else mattered. He continued on with his life like nothing happened.

John was in denial. Denial often becomes the active stage of "pretending" it's not going to happen, then going on with life as if everything is normal.

- "This is not happening to me."
- "I will not accept the fact that my wife is leaving me."
- "I will fight it with everything I have."
- "God wouldn't let this happen to me."
- "If I don't think about it, it will resolve itself."
- "This doesn't hurt me. I'm okay."

Never underestimate the power of denial. If the separation didn't exist in John's mind, then he was oblivious to it. Denial is an immensely powerful dynamic, making pain vanish by making it "nonexistent."

But John didn't realize that nobody walks through the fire of divorce without being burned. The emotional pain of divorce is real and so painful that some people try to ignore it or deny its existence.

Sometimes denial is the safest place to be. John didn't have to think about Ann not being at home any longer.

John wasn't aware that he was living in denial. He thought everyone else was crazy for not seeing the situation as he saw it; that "she would be back soon," and everything would be the same.

Sometimes during this denial period, people have a chance to think about whether they really want to go through with the divorce. Sometimes it gives couples time for counseling and to help save the marriage. But when one is living in denial, the preventive action is usually domination and manipulation, to force the divorce not to happen, to allow themselves to continue living in a fantasy.

REFLECTIVE QUESTIONS:

1. To what extent is denial a part of your grief process?

2. What are some actions you can take to move past the denial stage?

Asking for God's Help:

Lord, help me today to realize that denial is part of the grieving process. But living in denial only delays the hurt a little while. I pray that you will bring peace and healing to my troubled heart. Help me to acknowledge the fact that I must go through this process before I can become a thriving person again. Take away my fears, and help me to know that you are always in charge of my life. Amen.

10

feeling preoccupied: acknowledging your child's pain

. . . After all children should not have to save up for their parents, but parents for their children.

—2 CORINTHIANS 12:14 (NIV)

John and Judy saw no way to save their six-year marriage. They had seen a therapist several times over the past three years but, because Judy wanted more from their marriage than John was willing to give, they separated and later divorced. It was a difficult time for both of them, but their children were also devastated. They were frightened and confused. Many parents like John and Judy are so preoccupied with their own feelings of anger and guilt that they have very little time to deal with the children. But if you have children, you also need to help them. There are tons of books and materials available that you can use to research ways to help you through this difficult family time. If you simply are not able to help your children at this time, find someone or an organization that can.

Begin by talking to your children. Gear the information to fit your children's ages and their ability to understand. Be honest and open, but speak with love. If at all possible, make sure your former spouse is there. Reassure them that you both love them and you will both parent them. Reinforce over and over that it was not their fault. Tell the children that the divorce is final. Admit that this is a sad and upsetting time for everyone. Encourage your children to express their feelings. Carefully express your feelings, being cautious not to overwhelm them with the weight of your pain.

The younger children may act out their feelings instead of talking. Learn to read these actions so you can be aware of them, too. If you are the custodial parent, understand that the children will aim their anger at you. And, if you are able, pray with them. Take everything, every concern, every feeling to God. If you cannot pray at this time, at least let them see you on your knees. Remember, your children are experiencing the same grief cycle you are, but with less control over the outcome.

Be on the watch for distress in your children. Young children may become more aggressive and uncooperative, or they may withdraw into themselves. Older children may show signs of deep sadness and loss. You may see their schoolwork suffer. Teens and adult children often have trouble with relationships and self-esteem. If your children do show signs of distress, therapy can be helpful.

Children of all ages seem to do better if they understand that both of you will still be their parents and will stay involved with their lives. Research shows that emotionally, children do best when parents can cooperate on behalf of the child. If you are the non-custodial parent, try to call or e-mail your children daily. Stay in touch so that you know what is happening in their lives. Ask questions about what they are doing. Don't fight in front of the children, especially if it is about them, because they will think it's their fault and will feel guilty. Make pick-up days and drop-off days as easy as possible for everyone. Let the children love both of you, and don't get jealous if they enjoy themselves with the other parent. If you need to talk to your ex-spouse, don't expect the children to be your messengers. Don't say unkind words about the other parent, because your children know that they are a part of Dad and Mom, so they believe that if you say something unkind about the other parent, you are really saying it about them. Most of all, remember that the children are counting on *both* of you to parent them and take care of them.

Reflective Questions:

1. How are your children expressing their feelings over the divorce?

2. What is your greatest concern regarding your children's visitation times with your ex?

3. How do you handle pick-ups and drop-offs?

4. What do you do for yourself while the children are at the other parent's house?

Asking for God's Help:

Lord Jesus, you gave me the most precious gift that I could ever expect to receive . . . my children. Hold them in your arms tonight Lord—they need you. Let them know that you love them and will protect them. Guide me in my responsibilities to them during this difficult time. Help me to see that even as I am suffering, they are too. Sometimes I need to put my selfish ways aside for a while for the benefit of my children. Help me to love their other parent for the children's sake. Be with me this night so I may sleep in peace knowing that you are watching over my children. Amen.

11

feeling despair: getting help

What strength do I have, that I should still hope? What prospects, that I should be patient?

—JOB 6:11 (NIV)

Deanna finally realized that no matter what she was willing to give up or do, Travis was not coming home to her. She had tried bargaining with Travis and God, to no avail. She realized that no matter what she did, she could not alter the pending divorce. Now she was living in blackness, fear, sadness, and despair. She was convinced that she would never be loved or love again. She withdrew into a cocoon. She stopped going to church, parties, and social outings. She ceased caring about how she looked or dressed. Deanna felt like the bottom of her world was dropping out. She felt like her life drug on, as seconds turned into hours, and hours into days. She was sinking into an emotional abyss. All her hopes and dreams were lost. She entered into a type of depression that left her feeling like her life was over.

Depression is like hitting a brick wall. All your hopes, dreams, and faith have run out and, like Deanna, you become exhausted. During the depression stage, some typical symptoms you may experience are changes in your sleep and appetite, lack of energy, difficulty in concentrating on simple daily tasks, and crying spells. You may undergo feelings of loneliness, emptiness, isolation, and self-pity. This is a dangerous time; you may want to give up and may even contemplate suicide. Please remember that you *will* get past this. If you have these thoughts, it is extremely important that you seek professional help *now*. Never be ashamed of seeking professional help or obtaining prescribed medication when you are grieving.

Friends and family usually don't know what to do for you during this time. You may merely need some space so you can readjust and have some quiet time. Talk to your friends and family and tell them if you want them to just come over to sit and listen, not counsel you. Maybe you want them to simply hold you while you cry. If they ask what they can do to help you, suggest they bring something to eat that you can heat in a hurry. You may not feel like eating right now but this way food will be available for you when you do feel like eating.

This is the time when you need friends to call or come over for quiet support, prayer, and just a "Thinking of you," "Loving you," "Hang in there," and, "This too will pass." Getting help to wade through this rough time is important. When friends and family grow weary of listening to your story, look for a divorce recovery support group. These people are, or have been, in the same space as you. They can truly say, "I understand." While you may think this is an unbearable stage, it is also the first stage of actual rebuilding.

Reflective Questions:

1. Underline the words that best describe your feelings this past week.

Angry	Bored	Hopeless	Lonely
Contented	Terrible	Violent	Miserable
Optimistic	Weary	Loved	Hesitant
Irritated	Nervous	Annoyed	Rejected
Worried	Respected	Impatient	Unsure
Attractive	Useless	Calm	Bitter
Phony	Tense	Relieved	Confident
Needy	Satisfied	Supported	Detached
Secure	Willing	Interested	Fearful
Terrible	Anxious	Misunderstood	Hopeful

2. What are some ways that friends and family can help you through this time of sorrow?

3. Make a sign to tape on your mirror that reads, "This too shall pass." Recite the phrase to yourself whenever you are having a difficult time.

ASKING FOR GOD'S HELP:

Lord, break into my darkened world. Hear my plea and answer me. Hold me in your arms and comfort me. Show me a way out of this despair. Give me peace this night so I may sleep and awake refreshed. Thank you for being here even though there are days I don't feel your presence. Help me to resolve this depression and be joyful again. Amen.

12

feeling rage: resolving anger

The fool gives full vent to his anger; but a wise man keeps himself under control.

—PROVERBS 29:11 (NIV)

Rose wanted Todd to hurt like she was hurting. She thought of all kinds of ways to hurt him, emotionally and physically. Her rage was so strong that she would stay awake at nights scheming to get even with him. Rose would call his house at all hours of the night and hang up. Once she found his car at a local restaurant where he was dining with his girlfriend. She was outraged at the thought that he was spending "their" money on her. Her anger erupted and she poured five pounds of sugar into his gas tank.

Another time she decided if she couldn't have him, no one else would, either. She took a large pipe wrench out of the tool box and threw it into her trunk. As Rose was speeding her way to his house, she noticed a police car following her. She slowed down, thinking that she might be going over the speed limit in the residential area. Then her thoughts turned to the pipe wrench in her trunk. Could he know what she was up to? As she turned onto the street where Todd lived, the policeman turned his lights on. Rose panicked, but slowly stopped her car. The officer came up to her window and informed her that one of her taillights was out and needed to be repaired. A sigh of relief came over Rose. As she sat there thinking of what could have happened if the policeman hadn't come along, Rose realized she needed help to resolve her anger.

If you are in the process of a divorce, you will feel rage at some point. The extent of that anger will vary from person to person. Anger can develop so deeply and quickly that it can destroy your emotional well-being.

When you direct your anger toward your former spouse, there is no healing for you. There is only further deepening of the wounds, which can lead to retaliation. Handled properly, rage and bitterness can be used to provide motivation toward healthy and positive relationships. If you are going to use your anger for anything, use it to propel yourself toward the goal of your own healing, growth, and learning—not toward others. Use it to give yourself determination to become a happier, stronger, better person.

How can you resolve your anger if it is erupting like Rose's?

- Admit that you are angry, not only to yourself, but also to the person who makes you angry.
- Explore where this rage comes from. Sometimes it stems from fear, sadness, or a combination of the two.
- Decide on some small steps you can take to resolve this anger. (Remember, it is usually fear or sadness that you are really dealing with.)
- Target your anger appropriately. Maybe you are really angry at being divorced—at the broken dream of being happily married forever, at the idea that you now have to return to the work force—not at your kids or yourself, or even your ex-spouse.
- Run the shower in your bathroom as a sound absorber, and scream or cry or both. Get it out of your system.
- Call a friend, family member, or therapist.
- Get a punching ball and beat on it. Or try using your pillow.
- Take your rage to God. If you are angry *at* God, let him know. It's okay to scream at him. You may not feel very close to God right now. That's okay. He created you and he knows the depth of the anger you feel. Take all your issues to God.

- Make a list of ways to help defuse the rage that you can look back on when you're angry (e.g., take a walk, call a friend, go to church, take a nap, etc.).

Holding on to anger is like grasping a hot coal with the intent of throwing it at someone else; you are the one who gets burned.

—BUDDHA

Reflective Questions:

1. How angry are you on a scale of 1 to 10 (10 being extremely angry)? At the beginning of every week, rate your rage.

2. Make a list of at what and at whom you are angry.

3. Write a letter to one of the people on your list above. Let them know how angry you are and why. This letter needs to express your *honest* feelings. No one will see it. *Do not send this letter.* It is written so you can express your angry feelings on paper. Burn this letter, and as you watch the smoke drift toward heaven, know that God will take care of your anger and you.

Asking for God's Help:

Almighty God, the depth of my anger is unbelievable. Sometimes all I see is red and the rage takes over. No matter what I do, I can't seem to control it. Help me to use my anger in a healthy manner. Right now I am so angry at you for letting this divorce happen. Please listen to me and help me heal. Help me to better myself and learn from this anger, not use it toward anyone. Amen.

13

feeling anger: expressing yourself

Be angry but do not sin; do not let the sun go down on your anger, and do not make room for the devil.

—EPHESIANS 4:26–27 (NRSV)

Tony handled his anger in a different way. He was always taught that a good Christian never got angry. So Tony tried to not express his anger. He kept it inside. He would pretend that every thing was just fine. This divorce didn't hurt him at all. He would just move on quickly and everything would be great again. Tony had no bitter feelings toward Carrie. He was a *man* . . . he could handle this without being angry. Why should he be angry anyway? He wanted this divorce as much as she did. But then one day he realized he was becoming more and more depressed. He couldn't function like he used to. He didn't want to go to work. He didn't want to go out with friends. Tony was physically sick more often than usual. And he just wanted to stay home and be alone most of the time. What was happening to him?

Sometimes anger is so strong and frightening that, like Tony, you may feel a need to suppress it, to force it down, away from any conscious thoughts. This can cause clinical depression. Anger that is not expressed and resolved is one of the primary reasons for serious depression.

Think of your insides on fire with anger. If you don't do something about that fire, it's going to explode when you least expect it or when you don't want it too. It can cause health problems: ulcers, heart attacks, migraine headaches, high blood pressure, etc.

Anger must be faced and managed. The fact is that anger will be managed in one way or another. You have a choice of either controlling it and growing because of it, or letting it control you and destroying you and the people around you. Remember, internalizing anger is *not* the same as resolving the anger. If you feel your anger is getting out of hand, you may want to visit with a therapist for a few sessions.

Here are a few productive ways to express your anger:

- Admit to yourself that you are angry.
- Say it out loud. "I am very angry at ______. I am hurt, sad, and fearful."
- Accept the fact that you may still love your ex-spouse and yet be so angry at them that you hate them. It may be part of the reason you are so angry. This is painful, yet very normal for someone going through a divorce.

- Make a list of projects you can work on to help vent the anger in a healthy manner (e.g., join a health club, go to night school, try a new hobby, join a divorce recovery support group, etc.).

- Do not feel guilty about your anger toward God. It is very normal to be angry with him. Especially when you prayed that this divorce wouldn't happen, you went to church every Sunday, and you tried doing everything he wanted you to do. Express these feelings with him. Rant and rave and cry out to him.

- Make a decision to forgive. Maybe not today, but someday. Give yourself time on this one. Decide on a date when you will begin to leave the past in the past and start to rebuild your future without anger.

Many Christians often have difficulty stopping their anger because they mistakenly believe that their faith does not allow for the expression of anger. The truth is that anger is a God-given emotion. It is how you deal with your anger that may get you into trouble. Be constructive with your anger. Tony had many projects at home he wanted to get done, so he started working on one room of his house every evening when he got home from work. He would pound nails into the walls. He would paint and repaint. Sometimes he would work until two in the morning. But then he would sleep like a baby. Tony started seeing something worthwhile that he was accomplishing. He was turning his anger into something positive.

Reflective Questions:

1. Have you been repressing your angry feelings? What makes you think so?

2. In what way can you redirect your anger? Is there a new hobby, project, or activity that you could take on now?

3. How has your anger affected the lives of people around you (including your former spouse)?

Asking for God's Help:

Lord, give me the courage to use my anger in a constructive way. Help me to continue to work patiently with my anger and to express it in constructive ways. Stand by me when I feel so angry that I want to lash out at someone. Show me how to use my anger to accomplish things that I need to do. Forgive me for the times I've been angry with you, but let me know that you understand and love me anyway. Amen.

14

feeling furious: acceptable anger

And the LORD said, "Is it right for you to be angry?"

—JONAH 4:4 (NRSV)

When Mary Ann stepped out of her house, she would put on a smile, even though her gut was on fire. She was furious at Pete, who left her after thirteen years of marriage. In her mind she believed that good Christians, especially women, don't get angry. The message she received from her Catholic upbringing was that it is a sin to be angry, that Christians are called to forgive, and that they are supposed to feel joyful. If she didn't feel joyful, but rather had feelings of anger and resentment, she did not have a strong Catholic faith.

What Mary Ann didn't know was that the idea that Christians don't get mad is incorrect and impossible to maintain. The anger and resentment that Mary Ann was feeling was merely going underground for a period of time, and it would show up in other behaviors and attitudes which would likely be more harmful than the anger itself. Mary Ann tried to block out her anger, which made it impossible for her to remain emotionally healthy and well balanced. God intends for us to feel the emotions that he created in us.

Mary Ann lived in denial. Mary Ann claimed to be a good Christian women because she "was not angry," but she refused to allow Pete to see the children. She always had some excuse. But during all this, Mary Ann was smiling and volunteering at her church. She might have been saying that she was not furious with Pete but her actions contradicted her words.

In Ephesians 4:26, Paul says, "Be angry. But don't sin." What Paul is saying is that if you are angry, recognize it. Express your anger, but in a way that will not cause you to sin. Remember, it is not wrong to be angry, but anger can be wrong if you express it in a way that is harmful to someone. For example, it would *not* be wrong for Mary Ann to say to Pete, "I'm really angry with you for leaving me." But it would be wrong if Mary Ann took a hammer to Pete's windshield to express her anger.

Gritting her teeth and smiling didn't accomplish healing for Mary Ann. It didn't make the problem go away. It didn't give her any more power over Pete. It just kept her pretending everything was fine, resulting in Mary Ann "blowing up" at the kids or at her friends. Sometimes she felt like a pressurized can that could explode at any given time.

Once Mary Ann admitted that, yes, she was angry, she got involved with a Catholic Divorce Recovery group in her parish. In the group, she learned that it was okay to be angry, and she learned how to express anger in ways where no one was hurt. Mary Ann sat alone and practiced telling Pete about how angry she was, not just for leaving her, but also for all the shattered dreams of their future together. When she finally came up with words which respected both herself and Pete, she confronted him. After many sessions, Mary Ann could constructively vent her anger at Pete. She learned how to communicate her feelings with not only her former spouse, but with everyone in her life.

Reflective Questions:

1. If, like Mary Ann, you were taught that being angry was a sin, how do you feel now that you know it is the action behind the anger that is the sin?

2. Are you angry at God because things didn't go your way in the divorce? How can you vent your anger at God?

Asking for God's Help:

God, grant me the serenity to accept the things I cannot change,

Courage to change the things I can, and the wisdom to know the difference.

Living one day at a time;

Enjoying one moment at a time;

Accepting hardship as the pathway to peace.

Taking, as he did, this sinful world as it is, not as I would have it.

Trusting that he will make all things right if I surrender to his Will;

That I may be reasonably happy in this life, and supremely happy with him forever in the next.

Amen.

—Reinhold Niebuhr, 1926

15

feeling guilty: realistic and unrealistic guilt

I will not leave you orphans;
I will come to you.
—JOHN 14:18 (NIV)

Mike felt that divorce happened to other people, not to Christians. Now that he is divorced, he feels so guilty. He probably could have worked harder to make their marriage work. He feels guilty because his children will be labeled as being from a "broken home." Even though he didn't initiate the divorce, he knows he made a lot of mistakes during the marriage, and even now, he shows his anger a lot more than he should.

Guilt is a common and deeply painful element for many going through a divorce. While you may not ever feel guilty, many do struggle with it. It is important for you to understand that this is also a stage in the divorce process. It is normal and natural for you to feel guilty, both for things you did and those you should have done. You may try to cope with your guilt feelings by:

- splurging on gifts to try to compensate
- ignoring the people, places or things that cause guilt
- escaping the truth by drinking, drugs, sex, or lying
- doing good deeds to erase the damage you've done

There are two kinds of guilt:

1. Unrealistic guilt is guilt you place on yourself.

   "I feel guilty because I failed to keep our marriage alive. I should have tried harder."

   "I feel guilty because I should have been home more so she wouldn't have been so lonely."

   "I should have stayed trim and fit for him."

These are not the reasons why your marriage failed. In unrealistic guilt, your feelings of failure are usually based on someone else's expectations. You accept responsibility for all the unhappiness around you. Often you are not really guilty of anything, but you regret not having done *something*. It is the guilt of things you should have said, the things you wish you'd done, the "What ifs" and "If onlys."

2. Realistic guilt is something that you actually did.

   "I feel guilty because I left my family to be with someone else."

   "My wife left me because I drank and would abuse her. I feel guilty that I didn't get help."

You had control over your actions but you chose not to act. You *were* responsible for the break up of your marriage.

When allowed to be a controlling factor, guilt is a negative force in your life. You may allow the guilt to be an obsession, leaving you unable to grow through this stage. If the guilt is realistic, you must own up to it and seek help in dealing with it. Take a good look at the cause of your guilt (alcohol), accept responsibility for your actions, (yes I did get drunk and beat my wife), and then cleanse the wound (go to AA, stop drinking, ask God's forgiveness, apologize to your former spouse and ask for their forgiveness). Accepting yourself as a human being with frailties is another important aspect of getting beyond your guilt. Remember we all fail sometimes; but you don't need to wallow in it.

Reflective Questions:

1. Name the guilt you are feeling. Is that guilt realistic or unrealistic?

2. How do you usually react when you are feeling guilty (e.g., angry, silent, lash out)?

3. Do you put guilt on your ex-spouse? How?

4. If your guilt is realistic, how can you make amends?

Asking for God's Help:

Loving Father, show me if the guilt that I am feeling is realistic or unrealistic. If it is unrealistic, help me to move pass these feelings of "I should have," and concentrate on forgiving myself. If it is realistic, make evident to me ways that I can make amends with those I hurt. Teach me to know what is right and to practice it in every thing I do. Be with me so that I can grow stronger in both mind and spirit. Amen.

16

feeling grief: reactive depression

A new heart I will give you, and a new spirit I will put within you; and I will remove from your body the heart of stone and give you a heart of flesh.

—EZEKIEL 36:26 (NRSV)

Bob finally understood that Patty was never going to leave her new boyfriend and come back to the family. Bob was now a single parent. He felt guilty over things that he had and hadn't done during their marriage that could have caused Patty to find someone else. Bob had constant thoughts of worthlessness and hopelessness. He couldn't stop eating and spent most of his evenings in bed. He would have dreams of her coming back and loving him and the children again. Bob broke all ties with his friends and family. He had a hard time relating to the kids and spent very little time with them. When he did spend time with them, it seemed like he was either yelling at them or just letting them do whatever they wanted. Bob was showing some of the symptoms of being in the depression stage of grief.

Depression is a natural response to the death of a relationship. This type of depression is called a reactive depression. It occurs as a reaction to a specific event, like a divorce. How long this depression lasts and how intense it is varies from person to person. You may at one moment feel wonderful and be having a great time. Then the next minute you may be crying your eyes out, or, like Bob, be inappropriately angry at someone. This is normal. Some days or weeks you will feel like you are on an emotional rollercoaster. What's more, it is entirely possible to think you are over the depression phase because the symptoms have ceased, and have them return without warning when you see your former spouse again.

Be careful during this period to not use drugs and alcohol to "dull the pain." This only postpones the pain and can lead to severe complications. Having a social drink now and then is okay, but using alcohol or drugs to sleep or to get you through the day may be cause for major concern. It may make you feel better for a limited period of time, but it does nothing to help you through the healing process.

Probably the most common mechanism divorced people use to avoid their grief and depression is to jump into another intimate relationship. When your marriage is ripped apart, there is and should be pain, like when you go to the dentist with an abscessed tooth. The first thing the dentist will do is deaden the area around the tooth with novocaine. You will not feel the drilling that is going on at that moment. But when the novocaine wears off, the pain returns. Some divorced people think that if they find someone else, their agony will be deadened like novocaine to a nerve. But most relationships at this time do not last and frequently make you feel worse.

So what healthy methods could you use during this depression stage to help you with the grieving process?

- Get support from your family and friends.
- Try grief counseling.
- Start to accept the divorce and talk about it.
- Make small decisions on your own.
- Eat a healthy diet.
- Exercise regularly.
- Get enough, but not too much, rest.
- Learn to adjust to your new environment.
- Start taking care of yourself.
- Be gentle with yourself.
- Get help if you can't handle things alone.

The future is now up to you. Right now your future may seem hopeless, but it really isn't. You will heal from it in time and you will get on with your life. You will have a better life eventually because you will grow and learn and become a better person. That's what the grief process is meant to be . . . a growing and learning tool.

REFLECTIVE QUESTIONS:

1. Do you have any of the signs of depression like Bob did? Which ones?

2. Which of the healthy methods did you use or are you using now to get you trough the depression stage? Describe the results.

3. Draw a picture of yourself and then write all the feelings you are now experiencing around the you on the page.

Asking for God's Help:

Lord, in this time of sadness and loneliness, help me to feel your presence in my life. Help me to seek support in healthy ways and not through addictions. Guide me to properly handle things that come up with my former spouse. I can't manage on my own. Only you can help me find the right road to recovery. Lead me Lord. I will follow. Amen.

17

feeling stress: physical and emotional pain

I am with you and will watch over you wherever you go. . . .
—GENESIS 28:15 (NIV)

Norm was in the middle of the most stressful situation he'd ever experienced. Suddenly he was a single parent, handling all the children's activities alone, doing housework (which he never had to deal with before), *and* going to work every day. Norm was also coping with the loss of an essential relationship and a significant difference in his financial lifestyle. He had entered into the world of being divorced.

Norm used to laugh at the cartoon of a silly-looking man with his hair standing on end with electricity coming out of the ends. Norm understands that feeling; it is his life now. The heavy stress of divorce is wearing on him. This stress is not only emotional for him but also physical. Sometimes the stress gets so bad that his heart feels like its going to jump out of his chest. Is it any wonder that during this time in Norm's life he also suffers from other physical symptoms? He frequently wishes he could just lay down and die.

Feelings can be overwhelming while you are going through the stress of a divorce. Like Norm's, your body will frequently give you hints that something is wrong. Stress brings on overeating or no appetite, sleeping all the time or the inability to sleep, bowel problems, stomach problems, ulcers, migraines, colds, and the flu. All of this is normal; lousy, but normal.

One way Norm found to reduce stress was to take charge of his life. He took time to sit quietly and think about nothing, listening to music and using the tensing and loosening of muscles as a relaxation technique. He set priorities to spend time with his children, but also made time for himself. Norm learned how to say "no" when the request was not on his priority list. He started taking on one task at a time instead of looking at a long list and feeling overwhelmed. He started giving the children small jobs, like taking out the garbage and feeding the dog. In fact, the older ones started washing their clothes. He cut back on his caffeine and started eating properly. Norm made sure he got enough rest and took time for a walk after dinner every night. He started bowling again. He built close relationships with people who made him feel appreciated and important.

It is normal to be stressed out while going through a divorce. Remember, like Norm, you are more likely to be physically ill, so take better care of yourself. Divorce frequently leads people to finding or creating coping mechanisms, not all of them good. Carefully choose your methods of dealing with stress.

Reflective Questions:

1. Describe your physical symptoms of stress.

2. Write down four ways in which you can begin reducing your stress this week.

3. Take a week and don't worry about anything. Post a reminder on your mirror: "Don't worry. Be happy."

Asking for God's Help:

Heavenly Father, give me the strength to work through my stress and not take it out on others. Give me the courage to find productive ways of coping with the stress and keep me from taking the easy way out. Help me to not worry so much about the future but to concentrate more on today. Thank you for loving me and being here with me when I'm so stressed out. Amen.

18

feeling isolation: loneliness and aloneness

When you pass through the waters, I will be with you; and through the rivers, they shall not overwhelm you; when you walk through fire, you shall not be burned. . . .

—ISAIAH 43:2 (NRSV)

Gary would lay awake at night, feeling like something was going to smother him. He couldn't wait until morning to get up and go to work so he wouldn't be alone anymore. He would be exhausted, but at least he wasn't alone. Gary would hear jokes about divorce and he could hardly breathe. Then anger would overcome him. He felt so lonely.

Dawn felt most alone when she was around people. She would stand in a group of friends and suddenly realize that she was the only one who didn't have a "significant other." She felt ugly and rejected—a third wheel. She would see couples holding hands and start to cry. Dawn would watch TV until a romantic movie came on; then she would have to leave the room. Sometimes she would hear "their" favorite song on the radio and be so heartbroken that she would have to stop the car.

Dawn and Gary were both divorced and they felt the deep aching of loneliness. Everyone who goes through a divorce will at some point feel the heartache of being lonely. So what can you do about it?

- *Learn to like yourself, learn to be comfortable being with yourself.* Become your own best friend. Discover new adventures such as playing an instrument, taking long rides, planning a trip you've always dreamed of, begin new hobbies such as horseback riding or scrapbooking.

- *Help others.* Why stay at home moping around when there are so many people in nursing homes and hospitals who need someone to talk to? They are lonely, too. Schools, churches, libraries, and hospitals are eager for volunteers. You have to be a friend to make a friend.

- *Stop blaming others and start taking responsibility for your problems.* To start, stop blaming your loneliness on your ex-spouse. You need to find peace and serenity in yourself. Stop dwelling on who was to blame for things that went wrong in your marriage. You deserve happiness, so start making the right choices to help you find some. Live by the principle, "If I don't want to be lonely it is up to me."

- *Join a support group or take a class.* Joining a structured group or class will help you meet new people. But don't expect new friends to come running to you. You need to be a friend too. Make a commitment to talk to two or three people each week so your list of contacts grows. Don't give up after the first week.

- *Plan your time alone.* If you know you are going to be alone on a Friday night, stop by the video store and get two comedies and some popcorn. Get into your pajamas and enjoy the evening in your favorite chair. Or, plan a night to get caught up on your housework, do your nails, or read a good book. Have a plan in advance so you don't have a chance to feel lonely and sorry for yourself.

- *Exercise.* Get involved in an exercise program. Exercise will make you feel better by improving your health and lifting your spirits. This could also be an opportunity to meet new friends.

Loneliness and aloneness are not the same. Aloneness is a state of being, while loneliness is a state of mind. There are people who live alone and are perfectly happy, while others who are never alone still get that gnawing feeling of loneliness. Temporarily experiencing loneliness after a divorce is normal. There are two things you can do. You can allow divorce to take control over your life, or you can take control. Just because you are divorced now and are alone doesn't mean you have to be lonely. Think of things that you always wanted to do but your former spouse didn't. Now you can try them. What's stopping you?

Reflective Questions:

1. How do you handle your loneliness?

2. Has there been a time when you felt more alone than lonely? Explain.

3. What are some of the benefits of being alone?

Asking for God's Help:

Sweet Jesus, embrace me when I'm feeling lonely. Guide me in ways that will help me to meet new people and start new hobbies so I don't feel so alone. Help me to recognize that I'm never really alone, because you are always there with me. Show me how I can be a friend instead of always needing a friend. Thank you for standing at my side even when I don't feel your presence. Amen.

19

feeling afraid: handling fears

. . . Don't be afraid; just believe.

—MARK 5:36 (NIV)

It took Jack three months of separation and holding the divorce papers in his hands to make him comprehend that his divorce was really happening. Now a heavy wave of fear overwhelms him: fear of how he will survive living alone, fear of not seeing his kids everyday, fear of losing his business, fear of losing his Catholic faith, and on and on.

Fear is a major factor in the stress of moving on from your divorce. It is very important to learn how to handle your fears and get them under control so that you can get through your divorce recovery process. With the onset of the divorce, fears may start to overflow. For the first time in a long time, you will be living alone. And that is scary! You are afraid that you are not going to be able to cope with the challenge of divorce. You get angry because you do not know what to do or how to live in this new single-again state.

Financial insecurity is perhaps the biggest fear and stress of divorce. You may have had financial problems when you were both bringing home a paycheck. Now, you may have to pay support payments or get by on a single income. Your standard of living has been drastically changed. How bad is it going to get? How will you survive? Will you lose your house? All these fears pile up, but you need to realize that they are normal when you are going through a divorce.

You need to learn how to handle your divorce-related fears. If you do not learn how to come to grips with and have power over them, you risk losing your emotional and physical health. So how do you learn to overcome your fears? Reading this book and journaling the reflective questions is a good start, but here are a few other ideas:

- Find a friend, family member, therapist, pastor, or support group that you can talk to about your fears.

- Get your fears out in the open by writing them down on paper. Take a good look at them. Learn to face them. Consider fear your enemy and destroy it before it destroys you.

- Because the unknown is one of the greatest fears of a divorced person, you should counteract that fear by educating yourself about the divorce process. Learn what to expect in the next year or two.

- Know that most of the fears that you imagine are not ever going to become a reality. Think back to the last few times you were afraid that something might happen (for example: you won't have enough money for food, you might lose your job, etc.). Have any of your fears become reality? Most of them never do.
- Believe what Jesus says: "Do not let your heart be troubled or afraid" (Jn 14:27), and "Fear not, for I have redeemed you; I have called you by name; you are mine" (Is 43:1). During the early stages of divorce, this may be hard to accept, but just keep asking Jesus to help you believe it. Give God a chance. Don't be afraid that he is angry with you. He loves you and understands your fears.
- Understand that if you are Catholic, you are still welcome in the Church and may receive the sacraments.
- Repeat out loud, over and over, "My new life is not controlled by fear."
- Don't wait until the end of your divorce process to try new things. Don't let fear stand between you and your ability to explore this new world of being single.
- Know that overcoming your fears is going to take time. Be patient with yourself.
- Finally, *don't give up* on yourself or God.

REFLECTIVE QUESTIONS:

1. What is your worst fear right now?

2. How can you face this fear?

3. Who can you talk openly and honestly with about your fears? Why?

4. Write down each fear you have experienced as the result of your divorce.

ASKING FOR GOD'S HELP:

Loving God, I'm so afraid of being alone for the rest of my life. I'm afraid that no one will love me again. Help me to face my fears. I'm confident that with your help everything will be alright. Everything will fall into place. Thank you for being here with me throughout this most difficult time. Thank you for knowing me and accepting me as I am. Amen.

20

feeling resentment: deciding to forgive

And forgive us our debts, as we also have forgiven our debtors.

—MATTHEW 6:12 (NRSV)

Gary doesn't see how he could ever forgive June. She hurt him so badly. She not only stuck a knife in his heart, but she twisted it, again and again. How can he forgive June, when he feels so much resentment? How can he forgive himself for all the bitter words that he has said to her? How can he ask forgiveness of his children for the pain that they are going through? How can he forgive *God* for letting this divorce happen to his family? Is it possible for God to forgive all the agony and heartache that has piled up in him all these years?

It is hard to forgive. Sometimes it is so hard you try to avoid it. Usually, continuing to resent your ex-spouse ends up harming you far more. Forgiveness is a decision, not a feeling. But don't think that you are going to just wake up one day and decide to forgive your ex. It will take many months and, in some cases, years before the capacity for forgiveness becomes a reality in your life.

Why should you forgive?

- *Forgiveness liberates you from the past.* You may have spent a great deal of time and energy scheming against your former spouse (holding child support checks back from her, taking the children out of town when it is his visitation time, spreading mean stories about how abusive your ex was, etc.), but what has this accomplished? It keeps you tied up in the ongoing pain of the past. The more energy you give to resenting someone, the more your life is monopolized by that resentment. When you forgive, it provides your heart and mind the relief of moving away from the torment of the divorce.

- *Forgiveness breaks the repetition of punishment.* How many times have you lashed out at your ex? You know that it only resulted in retaliation, and then the war was on. Forgiveness is the only way to stop this cycle. At some point you are required to decide that enough is enough. You need to be the mature one and seek peace and forgiveness. "Vengeance is mine," says the Lord. Let God take care of the punishment. Please, for your own well-being, seek forgiveness and peace.

- *Forgiveness begins the journey of your healing and growth.* It frees you to spend valuable time, energy, and other resources on forming new relationships, creating happiness for yourself, and achieving personal goals. Forgiveness is necessary to move you further down the road on your journey to wholeness.

- *Forgiveness can be the easiest possible means of gaining personal self-respect.* You may believe, like many, that you would have more self-respect if you hit back faster and harder. Can you really respect yourself if you have so much hatred for another that you are willing to be at war with them constantly? Wouldn't it be better to be in control, freeing yourself by the act of forgiveness from the bitterness that you feel?

One word of caution. Don't forgive too soon. You have to go through the *whole* process of grieving, anger, and guilt before you can forgive. It is necessary to forgive yourself and you former spouse in order to heal. When you are ready to forgive, do it for your peace of mind and self-respect.

Reflective Questions:

1. Are you ready to forgive? Why or why not?

2. Define what forgiveness means to you.

3. Jesus says to pray for our enemies. How do you feel about praying for your ex?

4. When you pray, "Forgive us; as we forgive those who trespass against us," what are you really saying to God?

ASKING FOR GOD'S HELP:

Jesus, it's so hard for me to forgive ______. I will try to start now, for you told us that by forgiving others we are forgiven. Give me the strength to forgive ______. Please help me to forgive myself and love myself again. Jesus, I also pray that ______ will find healing and peace. Amen.

21

feeling ready: the process of forgiveness

If you forgive others their trespasses, your heavenly Father will also forgive you.

—MATTHEW 6:14 (NRSV)

Three years from the date that her divorce was final, Wanda decided that it was time to forgive Steve. She had been going to a divorce recovery support group and really thought that she was ready to begin the forgiving process. She had condemned him for all the harsh words that had been said between the two of them, for his affair, for all of his broken promises, and for the nasty court battles that had been a part of the divorce. Yes, she had a legitimate grudge against him, but she knew that she wanted to be free of the past. Wanda wanted the weight of all the resentment she felt for Steve to be lifted off of her shoulders. She was tired of being angry every time he came to pick up the girls. It had been three years now and she wanted to get on with her life. She wanted to find peace.

If, like Wanda, you are ready to forgive, here are a few suggestions on how to begin:

- *Seek God's forgiveness.* First ask for God's forgiveness for your part in the divorce. Ask his forgiveness for the times you were angry, resentful, and hateful even though you may have had a right to be. Many times you acted in ways that now you are ashamed of and wish you hadn't.

- *Accept God's forgiveness.* Sometimes your guilty feelings get in the way of accepting his forgiveness. Think of it this way: When one of your children disobeys you or hurts you, don't you forgive them? How would you feel if they didn't accept your forgiveness? It's the same with God. You are his child and he loves you very much and wants you to be close to him. God always forgives you if you just ask.

- *Let go.* Full recovery from a divorce inevitably requires a great deal of letting go—of control, of dreams, of burdens. The moment you let go, everything changes. With fear and anger gone, you see your situation in a totally different light. You discover solutions you would have never considered. Letting go is like setting yourself free to move on with your life. Remember, letting go is a state of mind, not an action.

- *Forgive seventy times seven times.* Forgiveness is not a one time thing. It's going to take many instances of letting go of hurts to truly forgive. Christ himself told Peter it may take hundreds of times to accomplish forgiveness.

- *Realize that you had some part in the divorce.* Divorce is always a two-person situation. Accept your responsibility and forgive yourself first. Condemning the other person may be the easy way out, but in the process of forgiving, you need to stop blaming others for your part in the divorce. Acknowledge that you did the best you could at the time and forgive yourself.

- *Seek and offer forgiveness.* Seeking forgiveness from your former spouse can be very hard, especially if your partner left you for someone else. When you seek their forgiveness you are, in effect, saying to them and to yourself that you are no longer willing to spend your valuable time, energy, and resources dwelling on them and their treatment of you. Forgive them, for your own peace of mind.

- *Make amends.* The final step is to ask if there is anything you can do to compensate for your part in the divorce, for hurt you may have caused your ex-spouse, or even for any physical harm you may have cause. If your former spouse tells you where you can stuff your offer of forgiveness or restitution, that's okay. You have tried, to the best of your ability, to make amends. You are not responsible for your ex-spouse's reaction, but by doing this last step, you have accomplished a very important step in your own recovery.

Forgiveness is very hard in cases of abuse, alcoholism, or adultery. Act safely. In these instances you may not want to literally face your ex-spouse, but to accomplish forgiveness it may be necessary to write or call. Even if this is impossible, you can still forgive them in your mind. Picture them sitting with you; then ask for and receive forgiveness.

REFLECTIVE QUESTIONS:

1. What do you think is your biggest hurdle in the process of forgiveness?

2. Is it going to be harder for you to forgive yourself or your former spouse? Why?

3. Why do you think Jesus told Peter he needed to forgive seventy time seven? What is Jesus calling you to do in this passage?

Asking for God's Help:

Jesus, help me to love and forgive my enemies as you did. Empower me to forgive my ex, but also to forgive myself. Send me your spirit of love and compassion. Thank you for forgiving me for all the times that I hurt and abandoned you. Show me ways to let go of the control and give it to you. Thank you for helping me through the forgiveness process. I love you and want to stay close to you. Amen.

22

feeling compassion: single parenting and co-parenting

I will be a Father to you, and you will be my sons and daughters to me, says the Lord Almighty.

—2 CORINTHIANS 6:18 (NIV)

Pam was terrified at the thought of being a single parent. She heard that children from "broken homes" had many more emotional problems than those in a "whole" family. She didn't want this to happen to her children. Pam read everything she could on single parent homes. She visited with other single parents and sought help from a professional. She informed the school about her divorce, and asked if there was anything the school could do to help her children through this difficult time. One of the first things she decided was that her home was not "broken." Even though the other parent lived in a different house, she was going to make her house a home for her children.

Learning about divorce and the related problems your children will face will help keep them—and you—from the battles that may occur between divorcing parents. Keep the following suggestions in mind:

- Take a class or join a single parent support group. Ask someone in your church's office if the church offers any classes. Some counties have single parent classes. Contact your children's school and ask for any help they can give.

- Find books and articles about the difficulties you face. Also, find books you can share with your child.

- Enforce the fact that you are still a family, even if you are no longer married. And reassure them you both will always love them and will take care of them.

- Be good to yourself. Depending on your circumstances, your own emotional and physical energy may be low. You need to first take care of yourself before you can be any good at taking care of others.

- Be supportive, even if your feelings get hurt (e.g., when they come home from Dad's house and tell you how much fun they had, or when a small child wants to talk to Mom and they are at Dad's home).

- Allow the children access to their grandparents and other relatives.

- Communicate clearly and often with your children.

Repeatedly remind them that they were not the cause of the divorce. Inform your children that neither of you are rejecting them.

Even though you are no longer husband and wife, you are still parents. Both of you need to keep the children's best interests at heart. Talk to your ex-spouse about how you can become good, compassionate co-parents. Think about the following suggestions and come to a common understanding between the two of you:

- Develop a parenting plan that allows both parents reasonable access to the children.
- Stay involved with the children on a regular basis.
- Keep your promises. If you say you will pick them up at a particular time or take them somewhere special, then do it. Conversely, don't make grandiose promises just to get the children "on your side."
- Be reasonable and flexible about holidays, vacations, and other occasions.
- Make sure both homes have structure and rules that are somewhat similar.

The kind of family you have following your divorce will very much depend upon the course you set for yourself and your children. Allow God to heal the pain and restore your family. Don't just let it "evolve." Have compassion for your children. Go to church and pray with them. It will take some work to make your home whole, but your children are worth the effort.

Reflective Questions:

1. What is your greatest concern regarding your children?

2. Ask your children what their concerns are. Write them down here.

3. Use one evening this week for "family night." Play games, read stories, take a walk, or just chat. Was it successful ? Why or why not?

4. What are some positive aspects of co-parenting? What are some negative aspects of co-parenting?

Asking for God's Help:

Lord, help me and my children to feel like a whole family. Give me the strength to help my children when they are confused, lonely, or angry. Help me to show them how important they are to me. Thank you for the people you send my way to help me be a better single parent. Empower me to be the kind of parent you want me to be. Amen.

23

feeling acceptance: preparing to move on

He heals the broken-hearted
and binds up their wounds.
—PSALM 147:3 (NRSV)

Jane worked through all the stages of grief, accepted her divorce, and was ready to start a new life. She realized that everything happened for the best. She remembers both the bad and good in her former marriage. She has accepted her part in the divorce and has started the forgiveness process.

Jane went to a divorce recovery group for about a year and discovered many new and exciting things about herself. She now believes that there is a plan for her which at this point only God knows. She doesn't know what path God has in store for her future but she is willing to be patient and have fun and enjoy life once again. She knows that at this moment she is not ready for remarriage, but at some point in the future would like to start casually dating.

When you reach this stage of divorce recovery, make sure you have done your grief work first, or it will come back to haunt you, somehow, in the future. Remember also that it's perfectly normal to revisit stages from time to time. If you have children, you will continue to be in contact with your ex-spouse (school activities, first communions, graduations, weddings, etc.), and that's when the old grief feelings may show their ugly face once again. The good news is that you will not stay in those stages as long as before.

If you're a Catholic, once you've reach this stage it is a good idea to visit with your parish priest to discuss an annulment. The annulment process helps finish up the recovery of your divorce, besides giving you the right to remarry in the Catholic Church. It is a healing process for most Catholics.

During the acceptance stage, you may want to start dating, but please do so with caution. Some people may go to extremes when reentering the dating pool. Don't even think of remarriage at this point. There is a much higher divorce rate for second marriages, and it is attributed to getting married too quickly after you divorce. This is the time for you to have fun and explore. And for now give your time and energy to rebuilding your life, not seeking a new spouse.

Begin this new and exciting time in your life with dreams for your future. You now have a direction and a reason for living, so add a little spice to your life. Write down all your dreams and goals for your future. Then write down how you are going to accomplish them. Pick one thing on your list and go full speed ahead to make it come true. Taking action reflects that you are proceeding down the road to your new life. Do it with hope, power, optimism, and confidence. These new goals become the road map for your future. You get to pick the directions, destinations, and routes because you are in control now.

Don't feel that you have to go through this process alone because you are in the final stages of recovery. If you are in a support group, stay there; if you are seeing a therapist, keep doing so. Remember that everyone handles the heartache of a divorce differently; the same is true with recovery. It may take you longer than someone else, but that is okay. This is the time for you to get to know yourself again.

This is also a time to recreate your personal relationship with God. Take time to be still and listen to him. Pray and trust that you will follow what *he* has in store for you, not what *you* want. Find ways that allow you to best experience the presence of God (go on a retreat, go to Mass every day or church every Sunday, take part in a Bible study, pray daily, say the rosary, etc.). Do this as often as your schedule allows. Give your life to God . . . and don't take it back!

Serving others is a way to give back to all those people who helped you through the rough road you have just traveled. Begin by helping out at your divorce recovery group, maybe even by being on the leadership team. We all have gifts and talents which we can use to help others. Many newly divorced or separated people just need someone who cares and will listen. (Remember when you were there?) If you don't have a divorce recovery group, ask at church if they know someone going through a divorce who needs help.

REFLECTIVE QUESTIONS:

1. What are your hopes and dreams for the future?

2. Now that it is time for you to give back, what plans have you made to do so?

3. What are some things you are doing to get back into a relationship with God?

Asking for God's Help:

Sweet Jesus, thank you for being with me on this journey. It just about destroyed me. But you knew better; you were there all the time carrying me and guiding me through. Sometimes I didn't feel your presence but you were there. For this I'm so thankful. Help me now to accept harmony and peace in my life. Show me ways in which I can use the gifts and talents that you gave me to serve others who are in the heart-break of a divorce. I know you will be with me. Amen.

24

feeling healed: starting a new relationship

O give thanks to the LORD, for he is good; for his steadfast love endures forever.
—PSALM 107:1 (NRSV)

Bill explained to his buddies that dating these days is a lot different than when he was a teenager. His kids made fun of him because he was so nervous and scared—yes, a grown man, scared. All his old insecurities started to surface again. Four years ago his wife left him to further her career. He was devastated at that time and felt very unlovable. But now he thought it might be nice to enjoy the company of someone of the opposite sex once in a while. So he decided to begin dating. But Bill, like a lot of divorced people, had no idea how to begin.

During the grieving process, you worked on who you wanted to be. So, who are you now? Make a list of your good and bad qualities (you may need help with this from your family and friends). Take a look at what you've listed. Do you want to work on or clean up any of the bad qualities? You need to be able to love yourself before anyone else can love you. Then decide what qualities you want in a potential suitor before you even begin to date. This will help prevent heartaches and awkwardness later. If you find someone with similar interests, you have a good chance at finding a new friend even if love doesn't enter into it.

It will take time and a lot of patience before you can start to date. Have you healed from the hurt and bitterness? Remember the saying, "If you are whole you will attract whole people. If you are needy you will attract needy people." Hopefully you are a lot more healed now than you were when you were first divorced. Do not rush things in a new relationship, or fall in love with the first person you date. Give yourself time to see if your relationship has potential and if your feelings are real.

If you still have children at home, gradually phase into dating. Begin by going out with friends once a week so the children won't resent you, or the person you are dating, because you are spending less time with them. It is best not to introduce every person you date to your children. They may become fearful, insecure, jealous, and worried that you too may abandon them. Some children also get attached quickly and then, when the relationship doesn't work out for you, they feel rejected once more. The more often you do this, the less they will trust any relationship.

Do not start dating because everyone expects you to. It's okay to stay single if that is what you prefer. Many older divorced persons choose to remain single and do not date at all. They enjoy the company of many friends of both sexes and do not want to change.

You won't find friends or someone to date by sitting on your couch waiting for your knight in shining armor to burst through your door. So, where are you going to find them? Make a list of activities you would like to participate in with a date. Now look at that list. How many of those activities can you not do by yourself? If you are like most people, your list has only two or three things that you cannot possibly do alone. Start enjoying your new hobbies alone, and you will soon find that you will meet many new friends who have the same interests that you have. By becoming active you start enjoying life, and you may be surprised who you will meet while you are having fun.

Reflective Questions:

1. Do you feel you are ready to start dating? Why?

2. Think of your best friend. What traits does he/she have that drew you to him/her?

3. What traits in you do you think your friends are drawn to?

4. What precautions are you going to take in choosing who you date?

Asking for God's Help:

Wise and compassionate God, guide me in my decision to date. Give me the courage to step out and trust again. Lead me down the right path and don't let me wander far from you. Grant me wisdom that I will choose wisely who I date. Strengthen me by your Holy Spirit to move on in faith, trust, and love. Thank you for being with me and protecting me at all times. Amen.

resources

Antoinette Bosco. *One Day He Beckoned: One Woman's Story of the Difference Jesus Made.* Notre Dame, IN: Ave Maria Press, 2004.

———. *The Pummeled Heart: Finding Peace through Pain.* Mystic, CT: Twenty-Third Publications, 1994.

———. *Shaken Faith: Hanging in There when God Seems Far Away.* Mystic, CT: Twenty-Third Publications, 2001.

Barbara Coloroso. *Parenting Through Crisis: Helping Kids in Times of Loss, Grief, and Change.* New York: Harper Collins, 2001.

Kenneth M. Dimick, EdD, and Janice M. Dimick, EdD. *Child Custody: Achieving a Parenting Partnership.* San Jose, CA: Resource Publications, Inc., 2002.

Sheila Ellison. *The Courage to Be a Single Mother: Becoming Whole Again After Divorce.* San Francisco: Harper San Francisco, 2001.

Ginger Farry. *A Single Mother's Prayer Book.* Mystic, CT: Twenty-Third Publications, 2000.

Anthony Garascia. *Catholic Remarriage: A Workbook for Couples.* Notre Dame, IN: Ave Maria Press, 2005.

James Greteman,CSC, Leon Haverkamp, MSW, and Elsie P. Radtke. *Divorce And Beyond: A Workbook for*

Recovery and Healing. Chicago: ACTA Publications, 2004.

Dennis Linn, Sheila Fabricant Linn, and Matthew Linn, SJ. *Healing the Purpose of Your Life*. Mahwah, NJ: Paulist Press, 1999.

Patrick J. McDonald and Claudette M. McDonald. *Out of the Ashes: A Handbook for Starting Over.* Mahwah, NJ: Paulist Press, 1997.

Micki McWade, MSW. *Daily Meditations for Surviving a Breakup, Separation or Divorce*. Fox Point, WI: Champion Press, LTD., 2002.

———. *Getting Up, Getting Over, Getting On: A Twelve Step Guide to Divorce Recovery*. Beverly Hills, CA: Champion Press, 1999.

———. *Healing You, Healing Me: A Divorce Group Leader's Guide*. Beverly Hills, CA: Champion Press, 2004.

John Monbourquette, OMI. *How to Love Again; Moving from Grief to Growth*. Mystic, CT: Twenty-Third Publications, 2001.

Mauryeen O'Brien. *Lift Up Your Hearts: Meditations for Those Who Mourn*. Street Skokie, IL: ACTA Publications, 2000.

Joyce Rupp. *Inviting God In*. Notre Dame, IN: Ave Maria Press, 2001.

———. *Praying Our Goodbyes*. Notre Dame, IN: Ave Maria Press, 1988.

———. *Your Sorrow Is My Sorrow.* New York: The Crossroad Publishing Company, 1999.

Barbara Leahy Shlemon. *Healing the Wounds of Divorce: A Spiritual Guide To Recovery.* Notre Dame, IN: Ave Maria Press, 1992.

Anne Bryan Smollin. *God Knows You're Stressed: Simple Ways To Restore Your Balance.* Notre Dame, IN: Sorin Books, 2001.

Margolyn Woods and Maureen MacLellan. *Comfort for the Grieving Heart.* Allen, TX: Sun Creek Books, 2002.

Phyllis Vos Wezeman, Jude Dennis Fournier, and Kenneth Wezeman. *Guiding Children through Life's Losses: Prayers, Rituals, and Activities.* Mystic, CT: Twenty-Third Publications, 1998.